# WEST KENT COLLEGE

C

4

This book is due for return on or before the date last
stamped below unless an extension of time is granted

# THE FIRE PEOPLE

A Collection
*of* Contemporary
Black British Poets

■

Edited by
Lemn Sissay

First published in Great Britain in 1998 by
Payback Press, an imprint of Canongate Books Ltd,
14 High Street, Edinburgh EH1 1TE

The publishers acknowledge subsidy from the Scottish Arts Council
towards the publication of this volume.

British Library Cataloguing-in-Publication Data
A catalogue record for this book is available on request from the British Library

ISBN 0 86241 739 2

Design by JW Graphics
Printed and bound by WSOY, Finland

The title *The Fire People* is taken from a commissioned jazz-poetry piece written
by Lemn Sissay and composed by saxophonist David Murray. Performed by the
David Murray UK/USA Big Band featuring Lemn Sissay in 1996. The piece was a
tribute to Andy Hamilton, saxophonist, from Birmingham, England.

**The Fire People** is dedicated to May Ayim

# Contents

The obvious names of Black poetry in Britain are not here. There is no Zephaniah, no Agard and no Nichols. With the exception of Linton Kwesi Johnson and Jackie Kay, I want to bring you something else. I want to bring you the new generation of poets who are knocking on the doors of the publishing houses; the poets that are performing their words around the UK and Europe; the poets who are putting their words to music; the new poets, the raw, the fresh Black and British poets – The Fire People.

Lemn Sissay
Editor

# Rambo 3

October 1.
Independence day.

As a special treat, reforming us
to accept this great nationhood

we are shown a film in the
dusty, dirty execution yard.

The killing wall serves as screen
old bullet wounds freckling the celluloid.

Those who can recite the national anthem off hand
get a free cola; throw in the pledge and you get a bun.

Hours before the film, the courtyard echoes the
voices of hungry men learning them in rote.

Rambo 3. We cheer as Stallone
achieves in 3 hours, the impossible.

Defying and destroying fascism – But there is no
make-up, doughnuts for crew or fake blood here.

Prices are higher, time moving slower.
But them, we have terrible inflation.

Hearing us cheer at the chattering guns
on screen, explosions echoing our hope

and believing we are rioting,
a passing patrol storms the prison.

Sprayed like so much water from a hose
bullets chase our fear across the courtyard.

Trampling shame and dignity underfoot
blood runs thick with spilt cola.

"Eat this" Stallone says repeatedly as
the dead projectionist's body jams the projector.

Later, the body count is high; over
one hundred are dead – or dying.

From my cell window, overturned chairs
check each other in a complex chess game.

Not the laughter, cheering, Coca-Cola
or Rambo 3 – not even the brief gasp of hope.

All I remember are the screams of men in agony,
the curious pop of exploding flash, the stains on my shirt.

# Articles of Faith

Skills
learnt in prison are meant to
prepare you to assimilate on the outside

but what to do with
a disciplined anus that can hide a
sharpened nail, piece of glass or even pencil

how do you apply
the educated guesses; an ability
to predict who will live or die today

can you share or even tell
of philosophies and insights gleaned in
silent places of solitary confinement

And who will buy
the blood you sold pint by pint to guards
in exchange for cigarettes, Coca-Cola or bread

Your blood which they sold on to hospitals
private clinics, research facilities
and obeah men in juju shrines

who will believe
you can compose whole symphonies in your head
waiting the romance of strings and voices, because

here we are forbidden to sing.

# Concrete Memories

In an empty cell,
stone
worn
tortured
scalded
by tides
of warm blood
and water
petrifies their guilt.

Nicknamed
Kalakuta Republic
in some distant pain
by inmate or guard.
Techniques to extract confessions:
Tried, tested, proven.
Interrogations are carried out.

Teeth,
pulled from their roots
with rusty pliers.
Methodical, clinical; each
raw tender wound
disinfected by gentle cigarette embers
and rubbing alcohol
mixed with salt for extra bite.

Rusty
cold
barrel of Winchester
bolt action Mark IV rifle;
retired right
arm of imperialism.
Enema. Rammed
up rectum, repeatedly;
twirling cocktail
swizzle stick.
Extremely effective, they say
at dislodging caked-in conspiracies.

# Mango Chutney

*"Plucking mangoes"*
Sport for guards, soldiers, policemen.

Drunk, home bound from shift end
they stop at death row, choose casually,

lining us up against the wall scarred from
previous plucking, under that spreading tree.

Picking his teeth, Hassan, veteran of this
game, picks us off, shooting blindfolded.

Last rites, an unceremonious smoke
harsh, throat and lung burning.

Usually pure marijuana soaked in valium.
They aren't too good at moving targets.

Sometimes they tie us, binding to post.
Legs have a habit of giving out in the face of death,

knees kneading your shame into dust, your feet
muffling whimpers in the sand.

Tied there, you die in clockwork regularity
long before any shots are fired.

Guns spit, arcs of fire hit bodies,
jerking limbs drown in empty spaces.

Bullets dust your body apologetically; you slump
but hemp hugs tightly so only your head lolls

face hidden. Ropes cut fresh tribal marks onto
your body, weight pulling against them.

Untied, you crumble slowly to the floor; and leaves
fall in spirals to land on bloody corpses.

I never get used to the amount of
blood; bodies droop like so many flowers.

Eyes stare, bright and alive into
another world. And death becomes some men.

Others wear it shamefully; others still, defiantly.
Their protest choking, suffocating.

Looking on, you notice small details.
His trousers are torn at the groin. He has a

lazy eye which gazes crookedly
into your mind.

His crime? Maybe he said no in the face of tyranny.
Maybe he murdered. The point? We will never know.

Walking over to the bodies, Hassan kicks them
hoping perhaps that they were not all dead.

The problem with mango plucking is the fruit
falls too quickly; and harvest season is over far too soon.

Spitting he bends down and cuts their throats
– to make doubly sure – vermin are tough & cunning.

Judge, jury, executioner – Hassan, drunken
petty tyrant; lust, rude and unbridled

by gun and 27 allocated rounds of ammo per week.
And for me a simple lust – to live as long as I can.

"Let's go" he shouts to his friends; amid
much laughter and back slapping they leave.

"Who did they shoot tonight?" a cell mate asks.
"I don't care" I reply looking away " As long as it's not me"

Daily epiphanies bloom as angels walk among us;
the few; the chosen.

# Cain

I'm
not my brother's keeper
ball   n   chain
but baby
if you play abel
I'll be your cain
fratricide's my claim
to fame

count drac
precision bomber
of urban faeces
the inverted commas
around your suicide
helicop attack
genocidal maniac

I'm
white p o w d e r
white powder
whitepower
I met a morphose
in my ivory tower
whitehouse

I just killed
jimi   janis   JFK
lady day
OK
I'm
the white trigger fix
shot malcolm X
666
invisible letters
white lines
of urban decay   K   K

I'm
the H in the Haight vein
white high
back in 68
the smack crack
that attacks the black
widow stuck to the thread
of the web
of the welfare state
deadlock   bed   rock
sista streetwalker
caught in the wheel of fate
of a 69   9   9

I'm
pied piper
vampire viper
the thin white line
gonna make you mine

baby
they call me cain
don't take my name in vain

big brother
jealous lover
worship no other

# AJAX

Just spent my last tenner on white powder, trading
Charles Dickens' crumpled face for a fading

pink postage stamp envelope sealed with a loving kiss.
Supply and demand = business.

OPEN SESAME

Parallel lines deck my mirror,
my destiny mapped out by razor

blade, destination North South
in through the nose, out through the mouth

and it's that ski jump Winter Olympics 78 kick
time is flitting, flying, and it's magic.

My pupils shrink to a fullstop, minute,
my nostrils sprint and my mouth, mute

with soap begins its terrible grinding
dance and I swallow hard like it's a double brandy lining

the inside of the glass like stretch satin,
And I'm Alice, Ali Baba, Aladdin

in the fast lane on the fast stuff.
*Don't stop till you get enough.*

*Time streaks on roller skates faster than a double-decker bus*
*down streets decked with disco lights, paved with gold dust*
*to The Underground, the whizz kid's placenta*
*for the bright lights of the city centre.*

OPEN SESAME

I'm devouring the sad ads on the Northbound
till I choke on PENALTY FARE £10

and study the facades on the opposite seat
*Trainspotting, Crash* and *Deadmeat*

'Fly the tube', I'd rather take a plane
concorde, to be exact, high on cocaine

'High as a feather boa
70s fashion victim strangles tube controller

for going too slow' that's my mind
working overtime, nose to the grind

and the wages of snorting class ABCs?
a) calcium deficiency
b) warped reality
c) split personality

OPEN SESAME

Typical that the doors of perception are jammed
when the queen of the star-studded dance floor's in demand

*Time pauses meaningfully, mean*
*then doors part and time fast forwards, clean*
*up the down escalator and run*
*jumps the queue at Club 2001.*

OPEN SESAME

They call me Jax, though my real name's Eva
the whole of Jackson Five rolled into one serious diva

No.1 on the guest list, top of the charts
when I make my grand entrance, the sea of sequins parts

They're playing *Do What You Wanna Do*, my cue
cos a girl's gotta do what a girl's gotta do

*Do The Hustle, Le Freak, says Chic,*
*Shake your body down to the ground.* Then peak.

90s out, 70s in
dance till our bodies siamese twin.

I take a mammoth dab of uncut paranoia.
now I won't speak without a lawyer

and they're playing *Night fever night fever*
from the best disco album in the world, ever

yeah, the Bee Gees are the bees' knees, honey,
now there goes a man who turns drugs into money

but not tonight, I'm skint and sky high
and on a scale from 'disco' to 'psycho'
I'm 'get out of my fucking space or die'.

*Time pulsates at 100 BPM*
*into the small hours of REM*
*and the contracted pupils of the chemical class*
*need to download for the last dance.*

OPEN SESAME

Open secret. Most of this loo queue have succumbed
to downing uppers, down-in-ones,

don't-look-in-the-mirrors and don't-stop-
till-you-get-enoughs. Welcome to the sweet shop

where white light overexposes shady deals
and crisp tenners convert to cheap thrills.

OPEN SESAME

Toilet lid down, the dregs, a thin white line
lines my nostril and drug-fucked I'm bleached clean,
cloned, confused, fused. 5.59.

OPEN SESAME

*Time: 6 a.m. Time to unpick*
*sleep stitched lids. Time to get rich quick*
*or just get by. Aja, family lawyer from Nigeria,*
*leaves for her two-pounds-an-hour job as cleaner.*

6 a.m. Now 70s chic looks cheap
as I boogie oogie oogie to the beep beep beep

of a space invader machine, worn-out, wide-eyed
my chewing gum long-spun and tumble-dried,

an item of off-white laundry. Time to exit.
Bright light. Day breaks my spirit.

*Time: 6.30 a.m. Aja scans the tube ads, prays.*
*For only God the omnipotent can raise*
*her spirits in this London, her sugar cane*
*dreams drowned, choked by cisterns and chains.*

OPEN SESAME

I watch her ascent as I'm coming down
and midway, in this split second, we common ground,

merge, parallel lines, North South, split
personalities, converge, compound, commit.

One way ticket. That's the way I like it.

                    Cheers
                  to the not
                  so distant
                  past  They
                  always say
                  the first
                  sip is the
                  accidentally
                  falling in
                  lust period
                  Had we never
                  met each other
                  happened to fall
                  together entwined
                  I would not vintage
                  that bitter-sweet taste of
                  lips met over a glass of wine
                  experience ninesummersrolled
                  deliciously into our one green
                  bottle  Caressed by the waves
                  we went the way of all lovers
                  when tipsy swaying to the hum of
                  summer bees our lust dried up
                  ran through fingers like sand
                  We noticed one-another's faults
                  your eyes took on that half-empty
                  half-hearted all is over look
                  You laughed when my jokes were
                  serious I cried when we were
                  bodily united mentally untied
                  tossing on a grey pebble beach
                  desperate scraping the barrel
                  making it up only to quarrel
                  making nothing but memories
                  drew the whole thing out until
                  it was out of control finished
                  sentimental dust I relive it
                  annually smiling vacant over
                  a bottle of wine now it's over
                  past just like the other nine

# OJ

Once upon a time
justice turns a black eye blue
white wigs sit stiff
fit on grey heads
as black and white misprint
rape and race

Once upon a time
justice blinks winks at hate
fist fucks fate
without consent
strangles truth and passes sentence
in invisible ink

# Girl Chile

The chile could not deny her birth
people said it was of little consequence
enjoy de wild days until de mirror is bitter
and twisted every month. Climb dem trees like a
monkey, swing de bat, bat dat ball, but
remember you is a little girl chile.

Mammie had worried since she cleansed de
clot out of her new-born's mouth, cutting de cord,
sucking de air, slapping the chile so her lungs
could expand, trying to breathe good feminine social
graces into her hair, praying she had mammies
good hair and daddies little toe.

Nine months of reverent prayers & frequent
church going to have a boy chile, or break the family's
tradition of bad wicked girl children from birth, until
the mirror got bitter and twisted every month. Nine
months shutting out Grannies prophesies and chants
to get female genes out of de poor chile's soul.

"Nine months of you stomach so low is girl chile you having?"
"God! if so make this one different". But no the chile was born
to a long line of haunted, mad & unmanageable girl children.
Mammie trying to beat the badness out of her chile's soul, talking
bout not wanting grey hair before the mirror became bitter
and twisted each month.

See the wildness came from way back, when, one of the
great great great grannies was pregnant with some other
grannie, or longer still, you never know how the story does go.
Great great grannie pregnant & miserable. Every day is pure eye water,
cos she husband seeing Mr Singh's daughter Sita. To make matters
worse dey only flaunting themselves in front of her wedding ring.

Sita bold as brass only parading all day left right left right pass
de house, from day dawn to day break. And she only singing
young ting does tek wat ole ting cant hole, young ting does
tek wat ole ting cant hole. Till one day Grannie couldn't tek
no more. Grannies head get light, she nose start sweat,
she hands start itch, she blood boil, and fists clench.

She march out de yard to Sita's tune and beat the chile
till she black and blue. Now is Sita cuss Great Great
Grannie's chile plus she future children, she condemn
dem to being bad unmanageable girl children, until de
mirror is bitter and twisted each month.
Or is something so de story does go.

# The Library of Love

I was out of date and antiquarian,
you dusted me off, you're the librarian.
My pages were loose, I was unwinding.
You stapled me together, you're my binding.
Frightened to wear my heart
on my sleeve blurb,
too many nouns, you were the verb.
The end of my lines were well overdue,
you paid all my fines, you can renew.
I wanted to be a loan,
you took me out.
I was at a loss leader,
you're my proof reader.
When no one credited me, you edited me.
And when critics rubbished me.
You published me.
From the shelves below to the shelves above.
You're the librarian in the library of love.

# Dutch Courage

Waking in the bright sharp lust light of sobriety,
Your face looms like the night before,
And tastes like the apple cider sweet.

The bright morning crisp bird song,
And an overwhelming feeling of doom,
For in the room, you are not there.

But in my thoughts, heart and very clit root,
You buzz, incessant wasp stinging my poor hangover,
And reminding me you will never be there.

So, I wake sober and in painful love lust,
And cannot wait, so hope and trust instead,
To drink your face out of my head.

## Blue Cheese, Raw Fish and Olives

When I grow up I will actually like olives,
And understand the need for an early bed,
And why I don't have to finish the bottle,
And why poems don't have to rhyme…
Red,
Lipstick will suit and stay on my lips,
And I will walk delicately, elegant in high heels,
I will have credit cards and generously tip,
Wonder if the world is getting younger and know how that feels.

"Excuse me, Madame Lady" strangers will say,
Offering me something nice, perhaps a cake slice,
And I will reply in a grown up lady type way,
"Oh! No thankyou, that will surely suffice."
When I grow up, I will actually like olives,
And while putting cool cucumbers on my tired eyes,
I will eat stuffed black ones truly believing they taste good,
Like blue cheese, raw fish and all other grown up lies.

## How (Not) To Let Go Of
## What You Can't Hold

Young woman
Old girl
Listen:

When yuh ears hard
life does you
the hard way.

One time, she offered her hand
to a man who had none
who bit it off.

So, she offered him another one
and he bit that too
Which hurt.

She didn't have to be so kind
tho she admits her intentions were not
strictly honourable

She needed this man
to be less stubborn
more ambidextrous.

So she grew some more hands
in a pot on the windowsill
with patient care

and nuff entreaties
to the skies.
The earth split

and they stretched
dovetail digits like
2 fluttering fans

and after a while
nails sprouted too
soft and harmless

She watered them often
and told them things
secret even to her.

Finally, one clammy day
She brought the man
a gift of forgiveness.

Im cut im yeye
hard after her
and closed his face

The sweat-grease blistered on
his skin so his image
slid off her eyes.

Undeterred,
She gave him a hand.
He let it drop

Then kicked it with such force
it pushed over
table and chairs.

He jumped up
and down on it
like a cartoon.

She knew he was green
since he'd seen
the greener grass

And she was rolling
all around in it
merry as could be

And he wanted to play too
but guessed you had to be
deserving

And he was too scared
that he might be caught out
shamed one more time.

She said, fret not thyself
anyone's allowed
pleez play with me.

This man, her love
needed help, and if you can
you should

(that's what Daddy-Mommy taught her
though *she* didn't
go to church).

Then she gave him another hand
– she sticks to her guns
even when they're held to her head

He screeeeeamed.
Dementing through the room
like a pinball

Desperate to smash
the nuff nuff
womanlove

that guilt mudbath
that clung to him
spoiling his suit.

She understood too well
her name was not really
on his curses.

But he turned on her
and by her own hand set about
tearing her apart.

He uprooted her hair
stripped flesh from bone
tweaked her heart.

She had no more hands
with which
to defend herself.

While he hissed, you must
let go of what you can't
hold on to.

once
i had a funny little idea
to write a poem
using pretty words and secret thoughts
my head started to thump
limply at first
so that i mistook it for my muse
belting out hums of rapture
in the caverns of her otherworld

i wrote the words:
*once*
*i had a*
and the sinews of my neck
snapped taut
in consternation
and i yawned
– not for the first time lately
*funny little idea*

and that's when it started
the belligerent cussing of an old nag
– one of the fleet
whose steaming wound-stink
frightens little children –
gaining in filth and volume inside

                  my
                  innermost
                          squirmed
at the bitterness falling off her tongue
like a chain of daisies trailing from

the hand of a child at thought
she knew my name

**Who di fuck yuh tink you is, eenh?**
**Whattar yoo doin'?**

my heart
deaf to the violence
bogled to birdsong percussions
and crunchy dry leaves
*to write a poem*
*using pretty words and secret*
my head threw a tantrum
and red-mapped eyes
found no consolation
so i made another cup of G&T

**Who d'ya think y'are, eh?**
**I never saw such bloodclaat tuppidness!**

Words stuttered
from the dropper
stodgy
slow    *thoughts*
*my head*
rolled right off my shoulders
into a dark fluffy corner
between the fridge and the wall
where my fearful eyes spewed blood-drops of
naked shame
but i knew the drill
tuned in to Misster Montel Williams

and his pageant of grotesques
lit another cigarette
yawned

the poems shoots swallowed by
the sleepy black hole
forever secret now
while the hag rabbited
**call yourself a poet?**
**every fucker thinks they're a poet**
**– and their mother**
**Except, as you know**
**some of them are Good**
mashed down the frail little seedlings
I had so bravely harboured
once

For days
i stretched my lips wide
under the control of
the yawning
wasted
by the task of breathing
i took to my bed
where no Biros lived
and on rhythmless feet
my brain slept defeated
zinc and iron
no good

new/old soundbites stalked my dreams

*Blk girls don't write Poetry
             don't tell tales*

Yet poemwords form
like ancestors rising creakily
from the primordial dew
to sing a world fit for Aboriginals
too big for paper

*Bright girls secure their own future*

(cos no man ain't going to do it)
in air-conditioned offices
an hour for lunch
a pension for the afterlife
(if you can spite them that long)

*So shut it and the closet door, you little fool*

So i licked up lifewords
by blanket torchlight
disgorged them like a young girl
giving birth in the screening rain
kamikaze words swooping
slippery sentences seducing
tempting
tormenting
spelling out the destiny i deserve
making me sick

it was me or her
she who held the NO
i who cradled my me
to her surprise
for the first time
I called the old bitch by her names:
BULLYINGWICKEDNESSTRAUMATISINGCHILDDEFENCELESSNOTMYFAULT

        time to get stink
            wield the pen

*did not thump*

she gone

# Reggae fi May Ayim

*it weard ow life wid det kyan canspyah*
*fi shattah di awts most fragile diziah*
*ow histri an byagrafi kyan plat gense yu*
*an dem 'angst' an dem 'anomie' gang-up pon yu*

afro-german warrior woman
from hamburg via bremen
den finally
berlin

it woz in di dazzlin atmosfare
a di black radical bookfair
dat mi site yu
sweet sistah
brite-eyed like hope
like a young antelope
who couda cope

wid di daily deflowahin a di spirit
wid di evryday erowshan a di soul

two passin clouds you and I
inna di dezert a di sky
exchingin vaypah

but in di commerc a di awt
woz it fair trade in regret
in love an lauftah?

mi nevah know
mi coudn tell
mi shouda site seh

    tru all di learnin
    di teachin
    rizistin
    an assistin
    di lovin
    di givin
    organizin
    an difyin

dat di kaizah a darkness
did kyapcha yu awt
dat di lass time mi si yu
would be di lass time mi si yu
dat you woz free
fallin screamin
terteen stanzahs doun
yu final poem in blood pan di groun
dat soh sudden dat soh soon
you wouda fly out
pon a wan way tickit to ghana
gaan ketch up wid you paas
mongst yu ancestaz

wi give tanks
fi di life
yu share wid wi
wi give tanks
fi di lite
yu shine pon wi
wi give tanks
fi di love
yu showah pon wi
wi give tanks
fi yu memahri

# Teeth

This is X who has all her own teeth.
Her mother is horrified by this.

Look into her mouth. She still has them.
Perfect pearls. Milk stones. Pure ivory.

Not a filling, no receding gums.
X was a woman with a lively

smile. Since she was a girl. No dark holes.
Her mother wore, still does, false teeth. Tusks,

badly fitted, left something unsaid
– a tiny gap between tooth and gum.

Her mum's teeth, in a glass tumbler, swam
at night: a shark's grin; a wolf's slow smirk.

What upsets her mother now, oddly,
is this: X had such beautiful lips.

This morning the men broke in – 8AM.
X was wearing her dressing gown, white

towelling. They came wearing her number
on their arms. *Did you know*, her mother says,

*they taped my daughter's mouth to choke her*
*screams. They covered her mouth in white tape.*

The small boy pulled at the sharp trousers.
He was soundless. The big men flung him

into that grey corner. His voice burst.
He will stand there, that height, forever, see

those minutes grab and snatch and repeat
themselves. The men in plain clothes have claws;

they attack his mother like dogs, gagging her,
binding her, changing her into someone

else. He will watch her hands smash and thrash.
His hands making a church, then a tall

steeple. He crosses his fingers. Squeezes them.
His hands wet themselves. He is five years old.

He knows his address. He knows his name.
He has ten fingers. He count them again.

This is X who has all her own teeth.
Came to this country with her own teeth.

Soundbites will follow. Lies will roll
tomorrow. The man with the abscess

will say she had a weak heart. High blood.
Illegal. Only doing his job.

Fill it in. Write it down. Bridge the gap.
Give him a stamp of approval: silver

or gold or NHS, she resisted arrest;
there's your cause of death. On a plate.

She was wrong. Give her a number. Think
of a number. Take away the son.

# The Black Chair

Now I am inside the room
after all the dreaded waiting;
a woman is kinder, more gentle.

So you have me open my mouth;
I open it gladly for you.
Tiny mirrors, softly you tell

your assistant the language of ivory:
my vowels, my consonants, my country.
It is all unfathomable to me

but it sounds beautiful, rhythmical.
I could be crumbling, spotted with decay;
maybe need a filling, a cap, root canal.

My abscess is a mystery, a swollen book.
You tuck me up and put me to sleep.
My soft swollen gums are stroked, all red,

my tiny dark holes prodded
by one of your strange foreign instruments.
They lie at my side now gleaming

sharp as a family, smiling in a silver album.
I am laid back on your director's chair –
the pink glass of champagne at my side.

Every so often I rise for a moment
like a woman rising from a dream of the dead
like a woman standing up on a horse

to drink and swirl and spit and watch
my own frothy blood spin and disappear.
You say good, good, you're doing fine,

again, again, till your voice is a love song
and every cavity an excuse for meeting;
floss is the long length of string

that keeps us parted. My mouth is parted.
You are in it with your white gloved hands
I have not eaten garlic for weeks.

But you don't need to pull any teeth
alas, no molars to come out in your hands
no long roots, no spongey bits of gum.

We won't go that far. No. It's surface stuff,
really. Not nearly as deep as you or I could go.
You'll polish them. You'll give the odd amalgam.

You'll x-ray. You'll show me the photo.
I'll look at my own teeth on the white screen
They tell me nothing about myself.

My teeth, speechless.
Rootless pearls, anonymous white things.
I need you to tell me about myself.

Will the gaps widen with the years?
Do you know the day my grandmother died was hot, baking.
Can you tell I like sex from the back row?

I'd like it now, on this black chair that you move
up or down, bringing me back to life
telling me in a cheerful voice, I'm done.

And because he once said,
My belly was set about with lilies,
He set about to beat me,
And because he once said
My navel was a round goblet,
He turned my stomach.
And because he wore a collar,
No one suspected him.

And because I was unworthy,
He grew to loathe me,
And because I worked hard,
He despised my rough hands.
And because I was his wife,
I submitted to him.
And because I failed myself,
He punished me more.

And because he became angry,
I saw his fury everywhere.
I could feel the colour
Of his rage on my skin.
And because I was beaten,
I was moved out of my house.
And because I was battered,
I was driven out of my Parish.

For he is the Lord in the Lord's place
And I am his servant.
I am she who looketh forth
At the morning, fair as the moon,
Clear as the sun,
Terrible as an army with banners.
I am she who cannot stop
Seeing his raised hand.

Our black door has a white X.
Next door but one has a white X.

59, 64, 65, 62, 68, and, fresh this morning,
58. The red headed twins just turned four.

Our white X on our black door seems bigger
than 64. Two of us are blighted.

When I come home
the first thing I see is the white X.

I can't help myself.
Once I've looked,

I can't stop. Even inside with
all the terrible breathing

and the smell of the terrible breathing,
even inside, I still see X.

Last night, the shape of it falling asleep.
I don't sleep deep now. I sleep the sleep

of the dying's companion – fitful, fearful;
strange sudden still moments, long empty moments

and the loud breathless breathing.
I see X. It is the sign of the devil.

I pray for the breathing to stop.
I get up and watch my two shrunken sons;

outside the canny moon is hopeful.
Tonight, let them both go in one fell swoop.

And let me get that X off.
I've seen them come late with the black paint.

I want the X painted over *immediately*.
I want a plain black door again.

But 62 says, 'once a marked
house, always a marked house.'

Even after it is painted over
you will still see it underneath,

62 says, smiling the strangest smile.
'It won't go. It won't go.'

I looked and looked at 62
and all I could see was a black door.

62 whispered, 'You can only see your own X then.'
62 gripped my arm till it hurt.

I tell myself 62 has lost her mind.
Poor soul. But at night I hear the strange

sound of X crashing its awkward limbs
seeking the foreheads of my two dying sons.

X has a life of its own, I'm certain.
I hear the reckless, racy breathing.

I'm sweating now myself.
I'm losing weight. I can see our bones.

Our bones lying in the grave, silently arranged.
Our bones – one big white X lying on the black earth.

# Daring

Falling out of normality
by birth, escaping
peer-shaped destiny
as soon as the courage
came to walk.
Tracked down, still
running until
safe ground found,
after burning the terror seed
planted unobtrusively,
nurtured subtly with the child
programming silence,
domesticity, compliance.

After burning the terror
seed with spirit sight
the invisible scars
still taint…

Since then
all free-fall
peace temporary,
yet more flame-licked
chasms to cross,
skeletons carried
in crevices
who taunt, when the
world sucks at the breath
urging
*"Surrender… surrender… surrender"*.

Daring for me
was no choice.

## Drinking

One touch
headspinning as expensive champagne
bubbling irrepressible smile
exhilarating as the cork popping
promising sweetness
soft as Summer dew rain.

Skin
a sun-ripened plum
enticing, concealed flesh
commanding, immediate consumption.

I'm longing
to be the bare feet drawing
your juices.
The yeast
fermenting desire,
plumbing to the depths
to refine rainbows
of deliciousness
to share

making every year
a good year.

## Spider Woman

She spun the argument
with a thread
he could not follow

perfecting
the delicate construction

until he
unsuspecting

fell
entangled

to
his

gentle destruction.

# heart (w)rap

i strap my heart
tightly
bind it strong

tough
was how i presented it to you

how you questioned me
on what was in this strange parcel

first tentatively
and then held it in your hands
and feeling the warmth
and faint beat
you guessed

and since
have tugged at the string
i so carefully bound
in protection

how you teased open
layer after layer
unravelled it all
until it lay open before you

how you were repulsed
when you saw
the pale blood drained flesh

i too drew back

hardly recognising the half healed mass
before us
disgusted by the scars
you did not ask
in what battle they were won

but fled

"the faint hearted"
i whispered to myself
"won't inherit"

and began again
to bind.

## Silver Threads

Together we built a palace
mahal
domes and minarets
tiny blue tiles and mirrors.

Wandered
hand in hand
warm feet
on cool floors.

Ran up stairs to call
from towers piercing skies.

Rushed through gardens
pomegranates and white flowers
ruby sweet pungent scent.

Trailed feet in fountained water
and when night fell
argued how many stars
embroidered the sky.

Sari like folds from the heavens
to drape us
liquid blue chiffon
and silver threads

we lay and unthreaded.
How rich we were
silver knots
untied piled high.

It was whilst i was lying thus
stars in my hands

and the heavens
on my lap

that you left.
i searched amongst the reams
of transluscent hope
fearing at first that you had been smothered

or like a baby
choked on a silver thing.

i searched our palace for years.
Until
nolonger ours
it became mine

all hope lost
single voice ringing
echoes returned
thrown from wall to wall.

i gathered our treasures and hid them in my purse

silver bits
spangled love

proof that i had not dreamed alone.

Black elephants
jazz dancing
gold and red
grin
i imagine
they wave
as they pass the window
of my third floor flat
just in case they are
i wave back.

I'd never seen so much blood.
His face opened like a flower,
pomegranate red,
burst fruit, decaying.
Kicking him was too easy,
he went down too easy,
I've never seen a man fall so easy
and so quiet.
The world lost its tongue
as he fell,
silent as the bomb that kills you.

I wanted this.
I thought
I needed this.
Six days at the agency,
Clients sit there chewing my thoughts
cows at the cud
Think a good billboard
will shift any old shit
Sell my wrinkle cream
Sell my magazine
Sell the impossible dream –
They give you a week.
Jammy bastards.
Think they buy you with the billboard.

Hate them,
hate their eyes, their teeth
their smell.
At a match
I am their Hell
like Dante never saw it.
Sell that.

I need this,
to connect to something,
my foot to his face.
I wanted this,
I thought.
Until his face opened.
A dahlia.

## Body Memories (no 1)

Involuntary Re-Memory
Reflex Replay
Carbon Copy Emotions.
I do not feel the sun
But I see it
I can not hear the rain
But it covers me.
Sun and rain
Fill my pores
I could drown
Easily.
Smells
Sounds
Scenes
De ja Vu
I can smell his
Fist tearing through
The air
And home it's way
Into my skin.
I hear my hair
Being tugged at the root,
Pulled and stretched
Across the floor
The weight of my body
Follows behind it.
I see my consciousness
Fade in and out
Then flicker,

Hi Tech
Audio Visual
Shutdown.
I transcend myself
Flirt with
Near death experiences.
I watch in slow motion
The movement of his weight mass
On her body.
I absorb the texture of her existence
I realise that she lies
On abrasive grey
Carpet
Fibres of which
Work their way into her mouth
And cling.
My transcendental fingertips
Acknowledge the grooves
Imprinted onto her cheek
Of where his
thick, cold metal
Watchstrap has been.
Indented proof
Of forced contact
Against her skin
Against her will
I know that she can
Almost see the sun
When she twists her neck
Towards the adjacent window

And narrows her eyes
Staring directly at the
Glaring yellow light
So that she can create
Rainbows
That fill her head with
A riotous kaleidoscope.

## The future's so bright
## I've gotta wear shades

Raman Mun

You wear the *right* labels
You listen to the Sweetest,
Funkiest sounds
You skim and shelve the *right* books
The *right* icons are displayed
in your lounge
When I listen to you speak
The *right* words
Trip inarticulately off your tongue
When you look at me
Your *rightness* is
**BLINDING**
But Baby
I wear the Right
Discerning shades
and I can see right past
your
Bullshit

Inside of my body there's a war going on
Seemingly invisible to your eyes
Slashed, knifed in the back, cuts weeping raw
Trailing bloody footprints across your floor
I am the walking wounded

You step neatly out of my way          Boundaried
Safe in knowing whats 'your shit and what's mine'
Seemingly invisible to your eyes
Inside of my body there is a war going on
And the bodycount rises high

My deaths have been silent and unmemoried
Little girls with their mouths cut out plague my dreams
You step neatly out of my way          Boundaried
Trailing bloody footprints across your floor
You are the walking wounded

Inside of my body there's a war going on
Seemingly invisible to your eyes
Confronting you with your blood on my face again
You step neatly out of my way          Boundaried

Inside of my body there's a war going on
Seemingly invisible to your eyes
Slashed, knifed in the back, cuts weeping raw
Trailing bloody footprints across your floor
We are the walking wounded

a memory / has to / look back
       full circle / to recall itself
          its beginnings and / how it got to stay
                      with you / it has to keep
                         recurring
              so as / to never forget
        how it survived
        the middle passage
        travelled from the hurting
        hollow of an african
        enslaved
to the inner city
       wail and moan
          of urban
             descendents
displaced
inna dis
babylon…

into the belly of one body of stolen lives and restless spirits
came joy
       a woman called
                joy
and the boy the boy named stephen
tore the gag from her mouth
bit through the shackles
with the sharp knife edge of his rage
and the strangest fruit
hanging
from the maple tree

untied the noose
around its neck
and set its shadow
free

into the belly of one body of stolen lives and restless spirits
came orville
        a man named
                    orville
his mother cynthia
put her lips to his lips and
blew the medicated poison
from his veins
with the kilohertz
force of her pain
and the strangest fruit
hanging
from the maple tree
untied the noose
around its neck
and set its shadow
free

a memory / has to / look back
        full circle / to recall itself
            its beginnings and / how it got to stay
                    with you...

into the belly of one body of stolen lives and restless spirits
came bryan
        a man named
                        bryan
his sibling colin
soothed the bruises
on his body
with the healing balm
of his tears
and the strangest fruit
hanging
from the maple tree
untied the noose
around its neck
and set its shadow
free

into the belly came
                joy
into the belly came
                stephen
into the belly came
                orville
into the belly came
                cynthia
into the belly came
                bryan
into the belly came
                colin
into the belly came
                more…

and the strangest fruit
hanging
from the maple tree
untied the noose
around its neck
and set its shadow
free

a memory / has to / look back
        full circle / to recall itself
            its beginnings and / how it got to stay
                        with you / it has to keep
                            recurring
                so as / to never forget
          how it survived
          the middle passage
          travelled from the hurting
          hollow of an african
          enslaved
to the inner city
      wail and moan
           of urban
              descendents
displaced
inna dis
babylon…

original pages
buried under the palm tree
talking drums and kola nuts
left on an african shore…
from old time deities
to jesus as saviour
praise hymn praise hymn
bible in a suitcase
smelling of moth balls
and promise
migration from the village yam
to king edwards potatoes
giving birth
to a new cultural identity

omo africa

dye fast colour on the red white blue
it's funny so true
no matter how many times
they wash that flag
neither persil
nor stay white
and bright daz
can remove the melanin
there will always
be BLACK
in the union
jack

omo africa

british children of shango and oya
eat chips and red stew
gari and water makes eba
you taste with a knife and fork
food can bring you
a little closer to the sun
without having to board a plane
or feel the pain
the indigestible shame
of being so english
in the motherland

omo africa

perhaps repatriation is a dream
for inner city soldiers
learning proverb in the margin
IYABODE
mother has returned
repatriation
a going home
within ?

omo africa

bi-cultural sculptures
created from the tools
put down by the very first
mother father immigrant
that pot of gold was a lie
we know these pavements

are covered in
post riot debris
brothers sisters beware
new age missionaries come with
reebok    nike       convertible golf
gti's

omo africa

original pages
found beneath the oak tree
rum libation
on a hard wood floor
yesterday speaking through
the talking drum
the bitter taste
of kola nuts
mingling with cornflakes
and spirits in the wind
spirits in the wind
saying
you never lose
what you choose
to recall

you never lose
what you choose
to recall

omo africa           omo africa        omo africa…

## Soul Food

oshun pa the moon     sat in my kitchen     and fed me
pieces of myself     she said i could     take as much
as my belly could hold     oshun pa the moon
was a blackwoman     coming to me     on the crest
of an urban daydream     speaking in soul metaphor
she must've been     skirting     the edges of my
sub-feeling room     and let herself in  while i was
drifting     drifting away     oshun pa the moon
sat in my kitchen     and fed me     remedies i had
long-forgotten     a jar of fresh     spring water
peace coming to me     peace coming to me
in ever increasing     circles     a little bush tea
to calm the tension     in my troubled womb
a hand     between the navel     and pubic hairline
to reconnect     reconnect     i touch my belly button
and remember     this is where     my mother
first nourished     me     oshun pa the moon
sat in my kitchen     and fed me     pieces of myself
til i was     full...

## Ethnic Conditions

i took this ebony mask
out of benin
and brought it here
reclaimation
of my soul
chapters of me
unfolding
and in the winter
when i remember
there is no snow
in africa
on this side
of the equator
in the coldest season
for the oldest reason   ;   to belong
i rest my african head
against this ebony mask
and feel a sense of

limbo

a sense of time disjointed
subconscious recollection
of a language i had
do not have
perhaps history
will record me
as a hybrid   ;   british-yoruba    european-african
spiritual hiatus
cog in the wheel or
am i am i

a new story
unfolding
in

limbo

sins of the past have created
this psyche
and i am the loss
terra cotta faces
staring back at me
from the art history
of an alien
perspective
benin bronzes
encased in glass
could be me
an african profile
pressed hard
against the frost
bitten window
of a no.35 bus
from there to here
in

limbo

i took this ebony mask
out of benin
and brought it here
because the house

in which i live
is not africa
but here

omo jide child of jide
omo sola child of sola
mother father
tell me the yoruba word for…
mother father
tell me the yoruba word for…

i took this ebony mask
out of benin
and brought it here
reclaimation
of my soul
chapters of me
unfolding
2nd generation
3rd world child
in first world chains
chapters
of me
unfolding
unfolding
unfolding…

## Ora Pro Nobis

I can see adultery on every corner,
I warn you.
Like a dive into a Nirvana coma,
Remain a loner.
Loose lips of etiquette,
Talking too much shit.
Like a group of righteous jokers
Seeking *détente*.
One can take advantage of human nature,
Still they will be forgiven.
Despite this they flee,
From life's *Modus Operandi*
Preferring to beg for cigarettes,
Instead of money.
They lose their identity,
On the way to autonomy.

Who am I?

Lost in the pages of Homer,
Remains of calibre in character.
It's like pulling clarity,
From the dense of the mist.
By my watch,
Ten minutes torn from time.
Words create confusion,
Confused? So you...
Place the words of my soul down.
Take your abstract dictionary,
Define the poetry.
*Ora Pro Nobis,*
I gave birth to this,
The birth pains were excessive.

sniff.in . hitting . nasal . tunnels
streaming bitterness
taste this
comic book quota of Utopia


smoke.in the taste of u thru a Romeo Ÿ Julieta tragedy
CuBAN taste . bud .s. hit . me 2xs
"she.s got stars in her eyes"
im Deaf & Blind when i wanna B
c o m e
a little closer 2 my rear view of U
married under a hail of StAr LiLLys
I dO B do U love Me 2 ?
i.ve seen U thru Smoked glAss EyE liDs
we slid in2 obscurity
im Blind when i wanna B
c o m e   2 m e


u smoke cigars & i sniff white stars
im trampling lillys B4 they can grow in this valley of ours
got the taste of u seeping thru my toez
im looking 4 cover coz im coma.toz


i dream of being a writer
i am of old in.tell.ect
grew up amongst nature studied the Life of Plants & In.sects
g i v e s  u  a  f u c k e d  u p  s e n s e  o f  t i m e i n g
y.r smileing
& im writing in my sleep

each sentence complete only as I read it

. IT . MAKES . SENSE .

type face DeNsE but recogniseable

MORPHIC STILO

even in Dream.Time im conscious of my eGo

i am a writer so i should B retaining this

i sLip out of sleeP

loosing the ability 2 peep at words formed in the minds eye

EyE spy Some.ThING b.ginning with P

& i dream that this writer can type a Story

can re.cite this Story wid E.nuff PRivacy 2 B in.side the mind of me

with out having 2B the Listener who misses the point

Re.mixing the joint with a Critical . Analytical . Back . Hand . Across . The . Back . Page .

A jealous mind travller who 4got 2 engage in freedom of press

FRESHLY PRESSED APPLE JUICE & LOOSE ROSE PETALS

spelling i love you

i only did it 2 show [u] how 2 turn hate in2 love

he said a gift of yellow roses R a bad O>MEN when 2 r in love

ruB a DuB DuB  there.s ominous suds floating in our tuB

wash me lyke u used 2 baby


see . i never used 2 talk in my sleep

& i never used 2 b so hungry that I cld.nt eat

& i never used 2 toss & turn & burn & yearn 4 rest

& i never used 2 keep u so close 2 my heart that i cld fart a.Loud

& i never used 2 wrap y.r warmth around me lyke a shroud

guaranty me the ability 2 loVe YOU 4 who U R
not how far you can pusH me
GUARANTEE VALID TILL THE YEAR DOT .
full . stop
guess . wot
I dreamt I was a Prozac . Sleeping . Pill . Popping . Queen.
sniffing WHItE StAr LiLLys 2 help me dream
CUTting U in2 easy 2 digest strips
taste this
comic book quota of Utopia
streaming bitterness
taste this
im Deaf & Blind when i wanna B
& Dumb when my GuMs R numB
come

LIMITED … I MEAN … LIMIT … IT

IT BEING WHAT YOU UNDERSTAND

ITS REAL … SIMPLE BUT TRUE

I … MEAN … TRUTH … FULLY REAL

THAT IS WHAT I UNDERSTAND I HAVE … GROWN TO KNOW

FROM THE IN … SIDE OUT … THAT'S MY TRUTH

I KNOW WHAT I KNOW … SOME … THINGS … THAT I KNOW ARE

… FRAGMENTS …

NOT CLUES AS TO WHO I AM

I UNDERSTAND I MUST ADMIT

AT FIRST I QUESTIONED IT

LYKE …

WHY DO I ONLY LEARN IN TERMS OF FEELINGS ?

DEALING WITH THE EMOTION OF A SITUATION HELPS YOU MEMORISE EVENTS

CONCRETE … EVIDENCE …

LYKE … SOME … THING … TINY

A THOUGHT

LYKE … IF I COULD KEEP EVERY THING REALLY TINY

I'D MAKE MY LIFE SMALL … BUT BEAUTIFUL IN DETAIL

I LIVE SPoRADICALY
WITH THE ENERGY OF A MADD WOMAN
AND I OVERSTAND THAT ...
THAT BEING THE ENERGY SYSTEM THAT KEEEPS ME TRIPPING
I ... MEAN ... KEEPS ME TICKING ... OVER ...
LYKE DRINKING COZ YOUR BORED OF BEING SOBER
LYKE RE ... PROGRAMMING PROBES
TO EXAMINE THOSE ... MOMENTS OF SUPER ... SENSITIVITY
RE ... ADJUSTS THE ABILITY TO ... THINK ... IN ... SIDE ... YOUR ... THOUGHTS
ITS ... KIND ... OF ... LYKE BEING CAUGHT
IN AN ALTERNATIVE NARRATIVE
WHERE WORDS ARE AWKWARD
AND IDEAS ARE COURTED
BY THE FACULTY OF PERCEPTION
**TIMES'ed By**
IMPRESSION
SQUARE PEGS IN ROUND HOLES ARE COOL
FOR MALLEABLE FOOLS
BUT ENERGY ... SHAPE ... AND FORM ARE PROPERTIES OF THE ENTIRE UNI... VERSE
AND IMPATIENCE MAKES ME CURSE ...
WHEN I'M UNABLE TO FIT IN ... SIDE ... IT
IT BEING MY DESIGNER SPACE WITH IN THE PLACE WE CALL EARTH
DESIGNER SPACE LIES WAY ABOVE THE TURF
IM KEEPING IT ... COMPLETELY TINY
BUT VAST IN D.TAIL...

THOUGHT PATTERNS UNVEIL THAT
REAL ... MAJIC ... IS ... TRANSFORMATION
WHAT ... I ... MEAN IS ... IF YOU USE YOUR IMAGINATION
THEN WHAT IS PERCIEVED AS REALITY METAMORPHOSISES IN
TO IMAGRY/stroke/IMFORMATION
OVERSTAND IMAGE AS THE PROPERTY OF THE ENTIRE UNI... VERSE
IF ... I ... REPEAT MY SELF ITS COZ ... I ... DIDN.T REHEARSE
B.SIDES THIS ISN.T POETRY ... THIS IS THOUGHT THERAPY
STRAIGHT OUTTA THE IN ... SIDE OF MY OUTTA UNDERSTANDING
I THINK THERE 4 I AM
SIMPLY ... KEEPING IT RIDICULOUSLY TINY AND TRUE ... FULLY REAL
MAKES EMOTIONAL SCARRING LIMITED
LIMIT ... IT ... IN ORDER 2 DEAL
WITH THE NATURAL TIME LIMIT BY WHICH WE HEAL
STILL ... WHEN Y.R DEALING WITH EMOTION

WHAT U REMEMBER IS THE VIBE ... I MEAN ... HOW BEING IN ... SIDE

THAT/stroke/THIS PARTICULAR REALITY MADE U FEEL

THUS MAKING THE MEMORIZATION ... MECCA ... NIZM ... VITAL

IN TERMS OF Y.R PERSONAL HISTORY

I SEE ... THE ... NEED 2 RE ... MEMBER THE NATURE 2 RE ... MEMBER

THE SIGNIFICANCE OF THIS EVENT AS REAL ... IZM ...

BREAK ... DOWN ... OR ... DEFINITION ...

THE ENDEAVOUR IN ART OR LITERATURE 2 REPRODUCE LIFE AS IT ACTUALLY

HAPPENS

HENCE ... CONCRETE EVIDENCE

OF SOME ... THING ... TINY

A THOUGHT

SMALL BUT BEAUTIFUL IN D.TALE

I THINK ... THERE 4 I AM ... WATCHING GROWTH

ITHINKTHERE4IAMWATCHINGGROWTH

SOME ... TIMES ... I ... THINK .

i don.t wanna hurt my rubber sole
so I tip toe
call me a ballerina
i can see the heads of flowers from here
THE GRASS IZ WHITE
so I feed it     PEPPERmints

QUESTION:    where do ideas come from?
ANSWER :     stories . your . Stories . GIVE US  a story!

O.K. lets say

        Im an inspector of tales-that wag like tongues
        I like 2 laugh from the b.ginning 2 the end
        but you must first comprehend that this STORY ain't FUNNY
        IT'S A COMEDY
        so promise me-you'll laugh from the right part of your body
        & if YOU can't find YOUR humour it's only b.coz U don't LOVEme
        see-y.r nakedness iz the same as mine
        what light iz yours is mine
        *shine baby-shine*

u bore me . surely u can D.code these mandible motions that run lyke gums . detect . saliva .
saliv . ate . dialect . is known 2 refresh the parts other speech can not reach .
9 out of 10 linguists experience this

CHORUS "im curious *[do dum]* im curious *[do dum]*"

WAIT . you have a fantastic face . what a future you have aHead of you !
R U accustomed to the use of poetry . 2 uncover the uncertainty of how we live
Yeah . but dig . if I were not would YOU speak 2 me in plain ***Old English*** ?

and still face the truth with out the use of masks
some people R terrified of the future b.coz the present b.comes their past .
*fate sometimes casts a doubtful destiny*
*R U free enuff 2 question who y.r supposed 2B…*

THE CROWN CALLS TRAGEDY VERSES IRONY

**too bare ones soul is**　　　**TRUTH**
**AS IS MADNESS**
**LIES CAN NOT B WORN AS CLOTH**
**UN . LESS . U . R . A . KiNG**

CHORUS SING : "QueenDOME 4 a Script"

GET A GRIP　　Audio.ences were not created 2 carry storytellers bagg.age

REASON　　　: it's way 2 heavy . even if we divide the weight by the mindstate of 40 listeners

O.K. O.K. how far R you prepared 2 take A play
take this plAY
How FAR moThER fuCKeR !

see we the audience want 2 add . 2 your venture . GET IT ADDventure

RAUCUS
CHORUS
*un-block your ears and face your fears*
*in times blacker than these we b.lived in fiction as a source of meditation*
*such is the nature of creation*

I am a ballerina
pirouetting skyward
I am the blk pupil
teach me 2 see
iam opening
retina rhetoric clearing
tune in2 your sound systm

B.COZ

**... WHEN WORDS FILL THE AIR**
**PEOPLE LIVE WHAT THEY BRETHE ...**

AUDIENCE AT EASE

/u sound older/no/wiser/YEAH/u sound wiser/coz of your age I guess/
[ah ... bless]
and I don't wanna hurt my rubber soul
so I tippety tip ... I tip toe
ccccall me a ballerina
I can see the heads of flowers from here
the grass iz white
so I feed it peppermints

? Where Do Ideas Come From ?

## Tupac came to me in a dream...   Vanessa Richards

The first thing I
remember this
morning
is a six pack of
brown bottled
Budweiser
laying across a
brothers belly.
Culunk, culunk,
culunk, CRASH!
The necks were
smashed.
The smell of Polo
everywhere.
Now the cylinders
were used for
pressing records and
chambering bullets.
Expensive cologne
became CS gas
and all my dreamy
friends were choking
on $2 dollar bills
Thug's life shelf life
is over
before the sell by
date.

Anticipate increased
sales
and further debate
about life imitating
art and vice versa
or vices of verse
steeped in violence
begging the question
are we
the violated black
man endangered
or the violent,
dangerous black
man
in Big Brothers plan
of a Nignog cog in a
freemason's wheel
going round and
round.
Drugged, bugged and
armed.
Brother's think it's
their own free will
to master a failed
plan
make'em think they
getting one over

on the man.
Meantime the man's
over him the
wholetime pissing in
his face
and the minstrel
thinks it's
champagne.
Finds self worth
singing praise songs
to false gods of
brand names.
Living large like a
rap star
but you're taking the
rap, star
and we all pay
penance
for the original sin
of not knowing how
or when
to begin loving
ourselves
unconditionally
without the
Babylonian trinkets
that shine
like fools gold luring
men more

macho than manly,
more terminated
than timely,
more divided than
divine,
see we need
reminding
that divisions are
illusionary
diverting our
attentions
from the power of
our own dreams.
So rest a while weary
son
then go visit your
crew
while they sleep
Tell them stories
of the difference
between
dollars and sense,
possessions
and values
and which ones
are best
forgetting
and which ones best
forgiving.

# Icarus

Who has turned music into a virtueless reality?
Peddled by marketing men turned Machiavelli
diuretics are swallowed like holy water
by distended children of the Diaspora.
Disaspora, Disasterous…
Damn
a big mac daddy eclipsing
then packaging the light of a mother's sun.

Social scientist turns wordsmiths into blacksmiths
extracting iron from our blood with sonic tools
hammering so seductively shackles worn invisibly.
Anchored to headphones.
Enchanted, unsuspicious listeners.
Lured then lowered to new depths
hook, line and sinker by the song of the siren.
Believing familiarity to be the truth
Guinea's children become guinea pigs
at the bottom of the I-Just-Didn't-Sea.

When the shipmaster of the SS Rags to Riches
throws a rope
can we be sure it's to pull us up from
where he dumped us last time?
Where we desperately jumped to last time.
On the long road home where is the north star
and who is the trickster at the crossroads?

If in your father's house
he sells you a ticket to visit his palace
then shows you how to climb golden stairs
polished by the G-stringed Hottentot behinds
of your foxy tarnished brown sisters
do you climb brother climb to the top of the charts?
Who welcomes you in the land of false economies and smiles?
Anemic hands applaud your arrival
unable to catch you when you're pushed
from the Tip Top Dollar Club with an almighty shove.
You better believe you can fly!

The question is
can you bear to fly alone
long enough to outgrow a mistaken identity,
to outwit a chameleon enemy,
to outlive your aborted life expectancy?

## He lays on his back

He lays on his back
and lets me love him.
I ask only that he let me climb
the space that separates
my soul from his,
his needs from mine
and that my kisses can wash away
every real and imagined fear
that stands between us.
I trace our history with my tongue
till I come to the place
where the future waits.
We sing a song of praise
then I taste
the unparalleled myths
that have centred on this.
The legacy of
the black man's cock.

With his hands in my hair
I'm thrown back in time…
I see my love hanging
from a big old tree.
His nakedness
swinging in the breeze.
Blood can't pass
under a strangling rope.
His hands, his feet, his cock
start to bloat.

Ya, that's right
didn't ya'll know the last thing
a hanged man does
is get a full on erection?

This is the scene
that drives the mob mad.
They fear they really want
what they never had.
Earth bound and hell bent
they're left
while the cruxified return
to the peace of freedom
I watch my king ascend
and carry his seed. Our life in me.
Long shall we reign.
In awe and anger
the lost ones
laugh and jeer
but in years to come
the noose would be around
the necks of their sons
who'd be playing
at a sex game called
auto-erotic asphyxiation.
If a man can hang himself
without killing himself
he can have the most intense
orgasm of his life.
If he lives.

1994 conservative MP
found dead on his kitchen table
wearing nothing but
ladies stockings and a noose.
Chickens coming home to roost?
And always back to the horror
that wasn't a dream
but rather a very real
remembering.

Prompted by his daddy
Junior drapes a confederate flag
from my hanged man's staff.
Something to keep him from
having to touch my love's skin
as he dismembers
with a hunting knife.
Something to wrap him up in,
bring home and show
the little lady.
"This is what happends to niggers
who step out of line. The only
yella babies round this place
are gonna be mine"
He says this every time…

They take the shackles
off my feet so I can cut
my love down.
His body falls.

And there he lays on his back
while I love him.
I ask only that I can climb
the space that separates
my soul from his,
his needs from mine
and that my kisses can wash away
every real and imagined fear
that stands
between us…

i was sittin' in his loving
my private parts became stained

not a mad stain on a new t-shirt
　　　　but a redecoration
designed on a nerve that could
burn down the city of new york
in a prenuptial suicide

i agree to die another death
when our parting comes
i become the attending angel
escorting you to a shivering shakti

ask her for the milk you
tenderly took from my soul
ask her to tend to the waiting weeds
gragging on the outside of your mouth

i did not know then
(when i accepted your garden to tend)
that the very vines i let enter my scented ancient bely
would thrill me by way of a tickled womb
　　　　　erasing loneliness
　　　　　projecting dynasties
　　　　　on the fleshy walls

when did you become scared of the mirror i held up to your heart?

I want to infuse
yo brew of babies

the tableclothe slipped
from beneath the cup

so here i sit
stained
by a simple man
a god to me
a boy to the truth

i shall love
trueboystruementruegodstrueboystruementruegodstrueboystruementruegods

you are that hybrid
me the young tender femme
thus
the infusion
the soul known
the drowning

the choice to sit in yo loving

## The Last Dance

I step in the party and vibrate
from late night bassline therapy.
Left my stress at the coat room
I've come to dance a wounded mind
before it bleeds insanity lead me to a dancefloor
to nod thoughts to the tempo.

Satin skinned sisters
boogie curves to a beat,
as brothers seek solace
in sexy sillhouettes
of hearts flowering in dark corners.

But back to my beat
Stylus sliding lyrics for my mind set,
grooves soothe the rest.
Ears suck soul notes for energy
Hi hats shift my hipbones
break beats shake my waistline
hearts and bass beats synchronize
and for four minute moments,
I am music

yeah,
I'm the ghetto lullaby
floating from towerblocks
caressing young faded heads
on the corner.

I'm the embraceable tune
of first time lovers
thumping funky rhythms
on a rickety bed.
Yeah, I am music
so I dance.

I dance steps
delicate as barefeet
on a broken glass mile.
Drowning in music
catching smiles and breaths on melody.

Dole queue blues drench my T-shirt
my dirty nikes stepping rhythm
from a month of tears.

DJ picks up the pace
and the place jumps and waves
hands swaying in the air
a testifying chorus of pain.
DJ flinging down commandments plastic.

Then music's spirit leaps
out the speakers
on a tidal bass
breaking on our faces.

Baptised reborn refreshed
I dance
I dance tears of sour sweet sweat
in slowly choreographed steps of death,
and the only thought I can hold is this tune
and if this party ends its too soon
so I dance, I dance
in clubs of dark damp grief
as hips of hurt sway some relief
I sream
I jump
I smoke
I drink
I groove
I dance
I dance
like this dance may be our last.

# Job

From the very first day I felt  odd
I mean as  soon as I  walked in the
office  the supervisor told me
aboutthe dress  code and tightened my
tie.till  I nearly choked,.For that  whole
month on my neck I felt a rope burn.

Six  months  on the photocopier
meant that the repeated searing
by those bright blue lights bleached my eyes
from a  subtle  brown to  clear  pool s of green.
Drawing attention from co-workers
who loved the change  Management smiled.

One year later constant exposure
due to management's new fangled plan
to make use of more natural light
meant that constant  exposure  of my
hair to direct sunlight bleached my jet
black curls  to a pale piss coloured hue.

Soon after that the  manager called
me in his office. He said that he'd
seen me grow he'd seen me change and
I definitely  look just  about
ready for promotion but I have
to prove it with my very being.

I worked day and night for the next month
on the office assistants end of
year report. I'll show him I thought I'll
get this  promotion even if I
have to sacrifice myself. When I
tried to print it  every word took

a corresponding chunk out of my
skin  colour. I stood there horrified
as the printer drained all my colour
word by word. I rushed the report
to the manager who took one look
at me and said the promotion is yours.

## On finally wiping the swastika from the bus stop

One more at the bus stop,
and London wears a swastika

it centres on me like murder.
no matter my amnesia it intrudes

like an unsolicited stare.
So who signs this evil art?

The leather-faced grandmother?
The pleated pinstripe-suited man?

The schoolboy in a rumpled uniform?
Or did one lay down its shape

to be retraced by the entire town?
You see it never seems to fade

since the first day I saw it,
it's just grown darker and darker.

# On the Tube

Walthamstow Central
Victoria line
& I'm scurrying
to Vidal Sassoon's Creative Hair Salon
to get all my nappy hair cut off

On the tube:
a young black girl
two exploding pigtails tied
symmetrical with red happy faces
Red T-shirt
On bottom red trousers
high top sneakers
pretty little frilly red gingham socks peeking out
& she writes
left-handed the scribble of the stops.
Her family:
attending brother
grandmother, dignified, holding baby
Directly across,
closed-eye mother leaning away in corner
& sweet new-born
fast asleep
in the stroller

Now,
all attention is turned
to Left-Handed-Young-Sister Red
    *T-o-t-t-e-n-h-a-m  H-a-l-e*
Brother-Overseer beckons
    *Have you done it yet?*

Young-Sister Red,
　*Yeah, man.*
Brother-Overseer,
　*Next.*

& grandmother tickles baby
while bored Brother-Overseer sends
paper airplanes landing on
the runways of people's feet

　*E-u-s-t-o-n*

& a blue-jean-cowrie-shell-wearing man
Right on the Beat
squeezes lips
to cop a glance
at the fine sistah
bedecked
in a positively surreal red shiny jacket
dazzling orange trousers, smoky almond
eyes, raspberry mouth, & most
pleasing cleavage
Nods
Nods
Nods
　*Yes,*
　*looking good*
　*looking good*

& grandmother
smiles & cuddles smiles & cuddles
smiles & cuddles & pats & strokes
& squashes nose to kiss
baby & sweet new-born
fast asleep
in the stroller

& another brother
sporting X
on a black baseball cap
& tiny
shiny silver earrings
that adorn
each individual
beautiful black ear
& elbow

elegantly poised
at the thigh joint
leaving wrist
& hand
to hang
silent
like a tear-drop
&

Left-Handed-Young-Sister Red
spelling out
the stops

    *O-x-f-o-r-d C-i-r-c-u-s*

*Heh, that's my stop!*

& I'm
outta here
scurrying
to Vidal Sassoon's Creative Hair Salon
to get all my nappy hair cut off.

## Migrations

There
are so many
poems of time
as I tidy
the living-room
carrying things
back
to their homelands

twice
three times
the fridge door
open/shuts
& ginger falling
on the ground
like a crush of velvet

& the soft
footsteps
of me
fairy-like
as if
I didn't even
live here
inside
this space.

# Fighting Juju

You danced the black/naked/black crazy
dance for God outside your yellow door
on a cold starless night and the Police brought
four of themselves to defy your barely
five foot two body of a gazelle
to twist your two arms, fighting Juju
of fire, love and hate and
                          placed
your black/naked/black self in
a cell for the night.

                Dreams
haunted you, weeds grew
from your mouth, your sentences birthed
dead earth crawling with worms.

You were tired, hungry and alone.
Who, came to you?
You danced, held out your arms in invitation.
Who, came to dance with you?

Then the air you breathed, frightened,
shaped strange, tightened its noose. Quick
sure, as fierce as a Diva's snap. And there were
no words left to say, no more dances left to dance.

We've all done the black/naked/black
grovel grunt on the death-earth crazy dance.
We've all had weeds growing from our mouths.
We've all lied about the place/s we come from
in order not to offend. We've all danced the dance
on straight time, in order not to offend. We've all
de-nap-fi-fied, de-funk-t-fied, de-nied and de-fied
in order not to/

                    Oh,
my little black gazelle
take care of your garden,
as well you should. Be careful
weeds don't strangle
the howling blues of your syntax.
Believe me, black is a horror
and air can tighten sudden
without warning.

                    Dance
your black/naked/black crazy dance
Dance it high Dance it low
Dance it with all your fight
and Dance Dance Dance
with your two arms fighting Juju
of fire, love and hate.

## Male Bonding

Sex Work Football Cars
Football Sex Cars Work
Work Cars Sex Football
Cars Football Work Sex

**neckgrip**

after the funeral
i found a box of photos

my mum had only ever shown me
old polaroids my dad had took
and her wedding album
                        full of the few
                        guests & had-to-be-there's

ie. those who kept their thoughts
about a black marrying a white woman,
behind their own curtains

you might call it the presence of duty

there are 3 photos in the box
all of them portraits
taken at some local photographer's studio

the props of the 50's, almost victoriana
and my father in his best suit
his neck and back rigid
in one he is holding a briefcase
in another he is pictured with a radio
in the last photograph, it is just him
standing against a dark curtained background
in his sharpest clothes:
all poses of affluence to be sent home
to give the impression of success

at home i remember
my mum telling me
about having to work 12, 14 hours in the shop
and the scraps she had to make meals with

## thoughts you would be embarrassed by # 1

some people really want the world
to be a beautiful place
they make consistent efforts
pruning & mowing and even
making a flowerbed
by the side of the road
w/bricks, soil & cuttings
from their own garden

where before it was just dusty pink gravel
there is clematis
and some plants whose names i don't know

she goes inside to admire her work
from the window
catches her son's eye in a photo
on her way to the kitchen
washes the soil from her hands
and goes outside to continue her memory
the tree was a lot smaller then

she hears the sound of play and looks
over the garden wall
and thinks paki bastards
at the 4 & 5 year old kids playing house

# Homeless

A handsome galleon Afrikan woman
skin shining melanin strength   hair ready to bind
told me one evening,   "You blacks in the west
(American, British) know nothing don't you know
what we call you back home?"

And she loaded her tongue and fired
"Niggers" she said
"We call you Niggers"

I guess she'd meant to hurt me
she was certainly angry,   indignant
at the alignment of racism
shoulder to shoulder with homophobia

And she threw the usual GIGO stuff
about *nature* and *choice* and *The Lord*
and seemed the most upset
'cause I wasn't effeminate

almost as if by *not* limping my wrists
I was someow being dishonest she said,

"It's different for you…
If you're Gay you can lie
If you're black you can't hide"

and,   almost in admiration,   I smiled
'cause for that moment at least
she was unique   colour blind

And because, in society, the soul is on the outside
and because, like her, I've nowhere to hide
she was angry, embarrassed, afraid because

*I   won't   lie*

# The Gift

You cannot give me freedom
I have always been free

These prison walls the boundaries
of *your* captivity

You fed the soil with my black blood
with my black bones you ploughed the earth

And now you say you never meant to hurt me
never doubted my worth
Well...

I will not forgive

and I will not forget

but we must live together or die foolishly
and so,   I offer my hand

if not in friendship then in hope
that your words are worth more
than your history

You cannot give me freedom
I have always been free

Freedom lives *in* me

# Roots

Elements of this discussion herald
my demise although the parts of me
no longer living are as yet un
noticed   as with music   not everything
can be written down

You home   your country
the country of the heart  home
is where that is they say   and often
affectation   till the solid waste assails
the rapidly rotating cooling device

Then the country of the mind becomes
the country of the soul and you recall
exactly where you left yourself
too late to struggle home (wherein
the slurry filled syringe persists)

as when
I thought you meant it when you said
*I'm leaving*
laid my continents to waste   important
wetlands permanently drained although
some pliancy remains   but now I am
the brittle man   have mercy please
and don't do that again

# Fair

I'll reign in then chain you in
I'll slit whip and rip into you
Till all the resentment cold as nitric acid
Pours out of my black chest
Onto your purpled curdled and blistered back
I'll whip you till you howl and crawl and cry
Pour salt in your mouth, rub shit in your eyes
Pour vinegar into the canals of your ears
I'll verify all your superficial fears

I'll wrench each finger from each joint
Till you get my point. Get it. Get my point!
I'll drag you by the roots of your hair
make you wish you were no-one, from nowhere
Show you what it's like on the other side
Show you what it's like on the far side
My knuckle dusted fists will rein down
Busting veins will curse,
blow after bitter blow
Then I'll ask you how it feels
I'm doing a thesis, I'd really like to know

I'll rip out your wifes' fallopian tubes
Cause there's already too many of you
I'll make you drink your own piss
I'll make you listen to this
One two three thousand times and more

Show you what it's like to know the score
I'll sell drugs to your children
burn down your home
Make you a stranger to your own
And what's more
The moment you run on fire,
through this poem, for the door
Gasping for air and some sense of pride
The same damned experience will be waiting for you outside

And when it dawns that this scorning
Is sworn in and government approved
When the pattern starts to emerge
And you're on the verge of enlightenment or madness
Immersed in the quiet violence of the day to day laws
When you notice the holder of the mirror has claws
And the reflection provided is disfigured and displaced
When your tongue splits on the bitter taste
When your head implodes
because the text between the lines
Is so suffocating that you've started reading minds
Then you can tell me that I am a racist
And we can continue our discussion
on a more equal basis!

# Advice for the living

Dead fast this
Everyones dying to arrive
Living for deadlines
Trying to stay straight as a die
They'll get there
Dead or alive
Cos they're dead set.
And they do arrive
In shores of dead heats
Dead beats at Dead ends
Dead messed up like deadstock
The living dead
Flogging dead horses
In the dead of night
dead right, dead lost
dead right.

every now and again
we stop dead in our tracks
dead still because it's dead hard
Like a dead weight drops
On your head
And you're a dead ringer
For dead loss

Wouldn't you die for a little peace
Die for a breath of hope
Dead right I would.
After all
In the dead centre
it reads
that Life is not worth living
If there's nothing to die for.

# Invisible Kisses

If there was ever one
Whom when you were sleeping
Would wipe your tears
When in dreams you were weeping
Who would offer you time
When others demand
Whose love lay more infinite
Than grains of sand

If there was ever one
To whom you could cry
Who would gather each tear
And blow it dry
Who would offer you help
On the mountains of time
Who would stop to let each sunset
Soothe your shades of mind

If there was ever one
To whom when you run
Will push back the clouds
So you are bathed in sun
Who would open arms
If you would fall
Who would show you everything
If you lost it all

If there was ever one
Who when you achieve
Was there before the dream
And even then believed
Who would clear the air
When it's full of loss
Who would count love
Before the cost

If there was ever one
Who when you are cold
Will summon warm air
For your heart to hold
Who would make peace
in pouring pain
Make laughter fall
In falling rain

If there was ever one
Who can offer you this and more
Who in keyless rooms
can open doors
Who in open doors
Can see open fields
And in open fields
See harvests yield

Then see only my face
in the reflection of this tide
Through the clear water
beyond the river side
I send you my love
And all that this is
a poem and a necklace
Of invisible kisses

If you can see the sepia in the sun
Shades of grey in fading streets
The radiating bloodshot in a child's eye
The dark stains in her linen sheets
If you can see oil separate on water
The turquoise of leaves on trees
The reddened flush of your lover's cheeks
The violet peace of calmed sea

If you can see the bluest eye
The purple of petals of the rose
The blue anger, the venom, of the volcano
The creeping orange of the lava flow
If you can see the red dust of the famished road
The white air tight strike of Nike's sign
If you can see the skin tone of a Lucien Freud
The colours of his frozen subject in mime

If you can see the white mist of the oasis
The red, white and blue that you defended
If you can see it all through the blackest pupil
The colours stretching, the rainbow suspended
If you can see the breached blue of the evening
And the caramel curls in the swirl of your tea
Why is it you say you are colour blind
When you see me

# Gambian Sting

A Gambian sting left her in Kwinella.
No money, no passport, nothing.
These 'brothers' know what to say, run it like
a pre-recorded tape: Play-pause-rewind,

no money, no passport, nothing!
These guys had promised overstanding,
said "Yes, Rasta sistah!" smiling at her
dreads. Said "Yes, you are home, in Africa."

These 'brothers' know what to say, run it like
a life line. Between me and the longing,
they read in my eyes. The restless ghosts
of unspeakable times, jostling for redemption

A Gambian sting. Left her in Kwinella,
at the base of a silk cotton tree.
Tears washing the red ochre, dusting her feet,
spirits thronging. To give salvation to the restless.

A Gambian sting left her in Kwinella.
No money, no passport, nothing!
These 'brothers' know what to say, run it like
a pre-recorded tape: Play. Pause. Rewind
the lash, the sting marking us both.

medusa: cuts both ways
dread!
an Afrikanwoman
full of sheself
wid dem dutti-eye looks
sapphire eyes
yes nuh! believe it
she could turn a man t'stone
some whiteman
night-mare riding
he mind across the centuries
in turn turning we mad

Blackwoman Medusa
dread anger
welling up in her stare
natural roots Blackwoman
loving Blackwomen
serious
he'd be frighten fuh dat
mark wid d'living blood
that bleeds and never dies
turns blood our sweet honey
from a rock
yes, that is sum'ting
would frighten any man
and still it goes on and on and on
around us inside us
their voices

whistling against
our thunder
across an eternal sky

Medusa is Nanny
Medusa is Assata Shakur
Medusa is Cherry Groce
is Eleanor Bumpers          is Audre Lorde
is Queen Nzinga             Saarounia
QueenMother                 is godmother
                            our mother
Medusa is our mother's mothers
                    myself all coiled into one

Medusa is spirit
Medusa in you is you is me

                    in me in you

Medusa is my shield
impregnable
my aegis
no mythical whitepeople shield
this is my armour
with Shango double-headed axe
Yemeja-Acuti
my battle dress armour
of serious dread

warm in a belly ole
out tru a mammy ole
into di worl ole
titty in yu mout ole
mess from yu arseole
tears from yu yeye ole
laughta from yu smile ole
eere roun yu precious ole
an in yu armpit ole
peayn roun yu nipple ole
tongue in you mout ole
an douwn yu troat ole
han' in yu bra ole
finga try yu draarse ole
love in yu body ole
tief in yu treasure ole
baby in yu belly ole
tearin tru yu fanny ole
nipple in dem mout ole
wipin dem batty ole
willy in yu pussy ole
joy in yu body ole
baby in yu belly ole
bursin try yu mammy ole
titty in dem mout ole
wipin dem rarse ole
love fi yu fambily ole
seizin up yu brain ole
centa ah yu life ole
fillin up yu ole

*life*

Part ah yu ole self
Nat all ah yu ole self
Yu is yu ole self
A *yu* own all wholes
Recreate yu ole self
Ram yu in yu ole self
Den open up yu laugh ole
An sing an laugh
An shout an dance.

# Fantasy

He was afraid not to study
>> because they said the blackman is lazy.

Afraid to be studious
>> because they said the blackman is thick and has to
>> work twice as hard

He was afraid to love
>> because they said blackmen are studs

Afraid to talk to me
>> because blacks always stick together

Afraid to talk to them
>> because blackmen are taking over their women

Afraid to rave
>> because that's all blacks are good for

Afraid
> to listen to his jungle music

Afraid
> to leave his racist black books on display

Afraid to retaliate
>> because blackmen are violent, are criminal

Afraid to fight
>> because no blackman-criminalman can be no lawyer, man

Ashamed
to
scrape their excrement off his bedroom floor

I cried for him, wanted to fight for him
They told me

        I was black … *wwwo*man
        that I would take care of him
        silence his anger with my breast
        dance with him endlessly
                the ancient dance
                    they said we knew best

        Let him swell my belly
        with a zillion little black
        taxpayer-aided lives
        to make him feel
        like
        a man again

So
I turned my raga up
loud,
doubled up what they said
            God gave me
            to stroke thick black throbbing with
The passion of my knotted kiss transformed
the thin straight lips to pulsing thickness they say
                is peculiar to us
I made them taste my breath:
*kiss my Black rarse!!*
and walked away
swinging it wildly.

# Auntie Magic
**(for my Auntie Enid ?-1989)**

I knew a tiny magic woman
who performed the greatest tricks
in all the world.
Her spells didn't work when she was big
for then they determined to climb her.
When she was small though,
they didn't even notice her and so her magic was
Most effective.

To love a man whose favourite dish
is thick oomanheart soup,
steaming hot:
Cook up di bickle
wid plenty peppa
An love im tenderly.

To raise children whose favourite game
is sucking
away the succulent sweetness of your sugarcane self:
Let di pickney dem chew and suck up your oozin' gold
to dry soaso yello
An love dem vigorously.

To live in land whose air freezes,
resenting your breath,
whose despising soil
melts itself to sink your light skip:
Gaze lickle sunshine tru yu Dunns Riva honey eye
to ease weh di hate.
Hum a sweet lullaby to rock it to sleep.

Chat an laugh lickle laugh wid di yawning shadows
stretchin tru yu empty yard.
Tell dem bout yu life
an bus two joke.

Kiss an hug up di people who mistake yu melodious mango smell
fah di faint stench ah peepee.
Smile at dem
so dem can see seh is stars in yu skin
not wrinkles.

No one understood her soft-toned magic
that took hate and greed and added herself to conjure
Beauty and delirious love.

## The Cultivation of a Sweet Tooth
**(for T.)**

He is so sweet
he thinks that when he kisses me
he will taste me all
despite the words he muffles daily
with his mouth
hooks out flicks softly away
with his clever tongue
shoves too deep to surface again        tonight

He is so sweet
he thinks that if he sucks hard
I will come all soft and chocolately
all rich brown fudginess
thick 'n' creamy

He is so sweet
he thinks that if he nibbles at this crisp dark outer
a luxurious brandy gold will run relentless
over his face,
drip hot round his mouth
sliding slowly down his throat
so gorgeous he'll do it again and again
till he's drunk on my stickiness

He is so sweet
he thinks that if he sinks his fingers to the depth of my centre
they'll emerge viscid from my easing fondant
They'll leave no whole to mark the passage

He is so sweetly wrong.

My insides are historical
ancient and crumbly
fine like dirt,
moist and warm like mud
all aglisten with delicate salt powder
he is so sweet
his sugar-hungry tongue is senseless to my shifting salts
he is so sweet
he won't admit to tasting
My sourness

0
  r
    e
   n
 e
  s
   s
    w
     e
      a
    t
   e
    a
     r
      s

all evidence of me all
those before and soon to follow

He is so sweet.
Like his father before him he may come to learn
that the cultivation of a sweet tooth
is a sad and dangerous thing.
I can't be

if I'm growing
I can't see
if I'm crying
I can't live
if I'm dying
and I'm dying

I can't win
if I'm losing
I can't cope
if I'm failing
I can't hope
if I'm dying
and I'm dying

I can't change
if it must be
I can't love you
if you hate me
I can't survive on misery
so leave me

I can't dream of tomorrow
when each day brings sorrow
this is why my laughter is hollow
I'm dying

## Parents

My mother washed clothes as a hobby
a virtue
passing long days upper floor Berkeley Street
Outside
men waited long shadows of themselves
in the light of the day
In silence they told of other places
where lampposts were tall trees
and traffic rustled four-legged through bush grass.
Cleaning up was a ritual that united my parents
washing up as he scrubbed down
her pinny, floral a bright contrast to
the navy blue-below-decks
where he sailed the seas
My father was ever restless
turning tidal in his search for a shore called home
every dock was temporary
every harbour a pause in his journey

This man came from rivers of stout fish
and escaped poverty to the destitution of manmade canals
where he never sailed in harmony with life
and so
She worried on his return
picking up pennies of labour
from a hand dirty with oppression
And feared
always
that one day he would simply jump ship
to join those still floating a middle passage
between here and there
and in the still night she would listen
as the sea wailed it's warning
*Once all of this was mine*
*Once all of this was mine*

## When I think of you
**(Malcolm Roy Andi d.16th January 1996)**

Tight as a fist
memory retains images of madness
corrupt days tempering intolerance
want and need competing

Torture forces fingers to spread
and reveal a space bright with colour
a coat hung on the wall
trousers over a lamp shade
and sunglasses worn by a book
unread and not needed
but literally digested.

Then angers or tears
and the fist closes
a hammerhead of strength
that no coaxing can relax

Sleep weakens
and laughter creeps out into the night
and smiles like full lunar
with all its insanity
now it is love time
and kisses flow as easy now as then

But grief wins over
and a tear like oil brings the dawn
and the light frightens the heart
making it flutter
and the hand of memory once again
rolls tight into a fist
to protect it from loss

# Christiansands

Always
What does that mean
Forever
What does that mean
It means we'll manage
I'll master your language
And in the meantime
I'll create my own
By my own.

## Hell is Round the Corner

I stand firm for a soil, I lick a rock off foil
Reduce me, seduce me, dress me up in Stüssy
Hell is round the corner where I shelter,
Isms and schisms, we're living on a skelter;
If you believe I'll deceive and common sense says you are the thief
Let me take you down the corridors of my life.

And when you walk do you walk to your preference
No need to answer till I take further evidence
I seem to need a reference to get residence
A reference to your preference to say
I'm a good neighbour
I trudge, so judge me for my labour
Lobotomy ensures my good behaviour

A constant struggle ensures my insanity
Passive indifference ensures
The struggle for my family
We're hungry beware of our appetite
Distant drums bring  the news of a kill tonight
The kill which I share with my passengers
We take our fill take our fill take a feel.

Confused by different memories, details of Asian remedies
Conversations of what's become of enemies
My brain thinks bomb-like, so I listen he's a con kike
(And as I grow) As I grow, I grow collective
Before the move sit on the perspective
Mr Quail's in the crevice and watches from the precipice
Imperial passage
Heat from the sun someday slowly passes
Until then, you have to live with yourself
Until then, you have to live with yourself

I stand firm for a soil, I lick a rock off foil
Reduce me, seduce me, dress me up in Stüssy
Hell is round the corner where I shelter,
Isms and schisms, we're living on a skelter;
If you believe I'll deceive and common sense says you are the thief
Let me take you down the corridors of my life.

My brain thinks bomb-like; bomb-like
Beware of our appetite.

## Suffocated Love

It's too good, it's too nice
She makes me finish too quick
Is it love, no not love
She turns me sexual tricks.
She says she's mine, I know she lies
First I scream, then I cry
You take a second of me, you beck and I'll be
She suffocates me.

Suggestion do you feel the same and maybe later on
I'll tell you my real name
She's so good, she's so bad, you understand
I can't stand, now I could just kill a man
She's on her knees, I say please
I cross her silly lies, she's got brown eyes.

I think ahead of you, I think instead of you
Will you spend your life with me
And stifle me
I know why the caged bird sings
I know why.

Forgive me you're forgiven
Kill the cur
Can you wait for yours I need to taste some
Life's really funny I laugh spend lots of money she's my freak
I guess I'm weak.
You ask what is this, mind your business
I pass idle days, with my idle ways till the twelfth of always
She walks my hallways
I keep her warm but we never kiss
She cuts my slender wrists
Lets waste some more time
I sign the dotted line
A different name: she-devil.

I think ahead of you, I think instead of you
Will you spend your life with me
And stifle me
I know why the caged bird sings
I know why.

She says I'm weak and immature
But that's cool, I know what money's for
Push comes to shove, her tongue's her favourite weapon attack
I slap her back
She mostly hates me.

Can I take off your clothes before we go out
And when you're helpless
I scream and shout
Sixty-nine degrees
My heads between her knees
You ask what is this mind your business.

It's too good, it's too nice
She makes me finish too quick
Is it love, no not love
She turns me sexual tricks
She says she's mine, I know she lies
First I scream, then I cry
You take a second of me, you beck and I'll be
She suffocates me.

# Talk to Me (Angels with Dirty Faces)

Someone talk to me now
Energy won't move me
Oceans won't soothe me
Cry me a bayou
Slime, sleaze pass through
You love it when I'm leaving
Angels with dirty faces disappear without traces
Them bones
Love it when I'm leaving
You love it when I'm leaving.

## merman

the day I married a merman, I led him down to the sea. said: swim as far out as you want to. and I waited.

caught him sleeping on city streets. I licked his shiny skin tasted salt on my lips. he said: I can't be here. this is not for me. the universe is not about this. I'm finding it so hard to breathe.

still, he loved me like a warrior. loved me like a child. loved me in petals falling.

the day I married a merman, I led him down to the sea. saying: swim as far out as you want to. and I waited.

days I could drink the sea. make you see me. knowing what would destroy you, would come right back and destroy me. so I sit by the water, as the sea becomes black and then blue, then black, and then bluer. I watch for a fin or a glint of silver skin in the distance.

tears come. I catch them on my tongue. it's alright, it's all right. the salt is proof that this was here. that you were real. that this was mine. and love is the constant essence of the waves. love, the constant essence of the waves.

the day I married a merman, I led him down to the sea. said: swim as far out as you want to, I'm here.

# Identity Hairpiece

Recurring nightmares
of a seven year old breed:
glacier advancing frozen slow,
over Crystal Palace Tower over
council houses at the bottom of the garden,
towards me petrified against bedroom window pane.

A sea of ice,
Croydon from Lagos.

That and bunches at forty.
Who could ever love me?
when there's no-one around who can fix my hair.
8 a.m. daily: facial skin stretching sessions
Post pubescent feminist grrls!
sport a goatee! Make your ears meet!
Make everyone think you're part Asian!
Got that early morning Sharpei feeling?
Visit Mrs. Odueki Wall – she'll set you.

Yeah yeah yeah – the only black blend family in town.
That old chestnut.
Raised on TV
mojos – three for a penny
blue-eyed blond haired envy and
chocolate milk. Ha, chocolate milk.

Avengers! Joanna Lumley! Purdy haircut!
Just like Mandy
Lovehateschoolmate.
Intensive creative visualisation manifested
months later into birthday present
"Ducali Salon" of Croydon High Street.

Entered hand in hand with my day at one.
Carried out in his arms at six.
Clutching a purdy to my skull.
From junior floor sweeper
to head head stylist,
the whole place bubble bubbled toiled troubled,
worked some serious white voodoo,
burnt and blew the unruly, uppity curls
to the North Pole
and back down.

Ever get what you want and feel
like you could die now?
(after they'd seen at school)

Regal and rigid,
bribed the evil older brother
not to beat me up/mess me up.
Hippy honky Daddy horrified!
Missing persons alert:
Have you seen this child?
Bogey picking-soap phobic-face stuffing – skateboarding
 – book morphing-halfbreed tomboy – Gone. Disappeared.

"It's a perfect evening for a swim"
Slab of subjective fact.
You don't have to put your head under"
Parents are useless liars.
He heard my "But-!" as a burp.

So I'm bobbing around the local pool
doing a really tense breaststroke,
neck as long as a cucumber,
twitching my way through the spray.

de de de de de de de de (jaws music)
Daddy Wall, 6 ft 3, huge hands!
Appears out of nowhere! Slam dunks
my purdy head down under
2 points!

As if it were that easy,
to get your baby back
from wishing to be like them,
older, wiser, winning.

For several weeks
I saw a purdy
on top of me.
Groomed a purdy
on top of me:
straight it was.
In a kind of bowl it was.
Blond it was.
White I was.
Like the others I was.

For a while,
nobody even tried to tell me different.
Moving moving moving so fast,
beyond race,
beyond childhood lies,
beyond the ignorance of adults.

Swimming swimming swimming
through glaciers.
To a secret place.
A wam breezy island where
I was special, mostest, bestest.

So I could make it to today.
Born again idealist,
rushing forward 'fro first.

"'Scuse me. Which way to the Curly Gates of the Afrodisiac Salon?
Heard it was along the path to enlightenment. Or was that schizophrenia?

## Freak Sex #2: The Dark Side
## of the Living Room Ceiling

Ya' dad's coming now
(and I don't mean down a long corridor).
He's riding your mother like Lester
bringing home the 2-1 favourite.
His body is drawn and tense,
waiting to spend the contents of his testicles
like a child inside the sweet shop where
the woman behind the plastic screen
won't serve him sweets quite fast enough.
He has a teethful of pillow
(the same providing handkerchief
for his sweaty brow)
and with the hand that's not
clamping her down
he's feeling her breast
in a vicious kind of way
as though it's detached from her
and attached to some page three girl.

Finally, the explosion:
it sounds exactly the same as when
his favourite cricket team wins
only deeper and more drawn.
He clamps her head down hard
one last time, and then collapses: it's over.
His mind can now broaden
from one channel (sex),
to one and a half
(who he's actually
been having sex with).
Only now does he figure he's been
making love to their ironing board –
does he turn away and think
of the price of petrol and MOTs.
As for your mum, she's been in a blizzard
snowballed by his semen.
She revels now in the safety of being forgotten.
Later it will cake round her vagina, that spunk
slip out when she sits and coughs on the loo.
Some of it will reach the intended destination.

This could be the story of your conception.

## My Mother's Porch #1:
## First Love at 15

I once kissed the pastor's son
on the way home from some
conference in Sheffield

I wasn't being Jezebel or nothing

but the way he asked me
so gently in my ear
if I would
if I could, if she wasn't there, his girlfriend

as though his love was bulging
through some prison he couldn't escape

I just found my lips
moving closer to his,
for that split second
of saccharin situation
of briefly requited love

and for that moment
there was only two in that backseat
our lips slotting together
just perfectly
and I was nuzzling in his arms
till that hour of Snake Pass love
was through with me

and then plucked
from the safety of his arms,
excited but unsure again

rooting around
on my mother's doorstep
for the keys

# My Mother's Old Coat #3

My mother has several of these
which she makes me try on
every time I go there
hoping I will fit into her old self
and take it places she has never been;
through the gates of divorce
and into new territory
She tries to sell me the antiques of her soul
in tweed and polyester and fabrics I don't recognise
and I place them down discreetly
as quietly I leave in a guise of my own.

The poems of **Chris Abani** in this anthology are based around his experiences as a political prisoner in Nigeria between 1985 and 1991. He was arrested after the publication of his first novel, which was subsequently considered to be the blueprint for the (foiled) coup involving General Vatsa.

**Patience Agbabi** is an internationally respected poet who featured in Channel 4's LITPOP series in 1998. She launched her first collection, *R.A.W.* at the 1995 Edinburgh Book Festival and is currently working on the sequel.

A pioneer of the present spoken word movement, **Malika Booker** has performed with writers such as Sapphire, Terry McMillan and Earl Lovelace, as well as recording work for Radio 4. She is editing an anthology entitled *In Our Lifetime* featuring poets from around the world and presently works as the Education Worker at Apples & Snakes performance poetry agency.

**John Citizen** is Liverpool born and thirty somewhere. An old school report quotes 'his reading improves and he takes trouble with his written work'. He can live with that.

**Salena Saliva Godden**. Hailed as an art school Neneh Cherry, Salena is known for taking poetry away from the classroom, chin-strokers and into club culture. Featured on Coldcut's latest album *Let Us Play*, she is currently recording her debut album.

She born in Kingston, raise in Bolton, learn in Bradford, live in London. Next stop: planet earth. **Lorraine Griffiths,** journalist and demon chaser, is working on her first novel. Give thanks.

Jamaican-born reggae poet **Linton Kwesi Johnson** has published four volumes of poetry and recorded eleven albums. His latest album *More Time* celebrates 20 years as a recording artist and puts 'Reggae Fi May Ayim' to music.

**Parm Kaur** binds disparate strands of kaleidoscopic cultures with filaments of fable, weaving glistening spellbinding webs which glisten across everchanging landscapes of time, catching lover's whispers and revolutionary screams.

Winner of the Eric Gregory Award in 1991, Edinburgh-born **Jackie Kay** is one of the UK's most renowned and respected poets.

**Shamshad Khan.** 1964 Introspection of introspection     inappropriate laughter     hurt
upturned     Identity writing **classes** on rainy nights     orange lights anthologies     Virago short story
publication     "Flaming Spirit" 1994 recognition     open heart performance     Radio 4
"Love Thang"     transfusion     Manchester Poetry Festival     mushiara learning expansion     Slams
Apples and Snakes     and here

Born in Washington, D.C., educated at Emmanuel College, Cambridge, poet, playwright, and singer
**Cheryl Martin** has had plays produced for television, radio, and stage. Previously published, her solo
collection *Buffalo Dreams* is forthcoming from The Word Hoard, Huddersfield.

**Raman Mundair**     indian
An urban griot
Creating kaleidoscopic images
woman
From the heartbodysoulspiritmind
In a landscape void
Of reflections of self.
Currently creating for Talawa and Tamasha Theatre Co. and Sankofa Film Co.

**Olubunmi Iyabode Abidemi Ejide Ogunsiji**, first daughter of Sola & Jide. Dualities, dichotomies in
me, in life and spirit, guide my hand, make the word… make the whole…

**Koye Oyedeji** was born in Greenwich, London 1976. His psychological poetry has already received
numerous positive reviews including a commentary from Patricia Scalan. He has recently completed
his experimental novel, a fusion of both poetry and prose, entitled *Tempus Machina*.

"As a writer I have always been intrigued with the survival of the human spirit. For me poetry lives
somewhere within that energy/space and time. The majic is to create Word Systems that take us
there." London based writer and performance poet **Mallissa Read**.

Brixton based and Vancouver born **Vanessa Richards** is a writer, performer, workshop facilitator,
and student of the Word. Canada's underground music and experimental art scene in the 1980's
nurtured the artist. She came to London in 1992 and combined her writing and performance skills.
With this history she continues to create work that is intimate, political, and focused always
on evolution…

Hailing from Los Angeles, **Khefri Riley** is a founding member of the Urban Poets Society and is now Producer and Co-Artistic Director of Mannafest curating various intermedia arts events. Performing as KA'frique she has shared the spotlight with The Last Poets, held cypher at The Anansi Writers Workshop LA, rocked the mic in South Africa, planted seeds in London's underground club scene, has recordings in London, Japan and Germany, and continues to dwell in spirit and freakmommadom.

**Roger Robinson** is a graduate of the infamous 'Speakers Corna' poetry jams at Brixton Art Gallery and is a former member of the now disbanded Urban Poets Society. He is presently co-editing a collection entitled *Generation Conversation* featuring a selection of young UK and US poets, while working as the programmer for Apples & Snakes performance poetry agency.

**Joy Russell** was born in Belize, lived in Canada and now lives in London working as a researcher in television. Her work has appeared in various UK and North American publications.

**Kadija Sesay** has edited two anthologies, *Six Plays by Black and Asian Women Writers* and *Burning Words, Flaming Images*. She was a Black Literature Development Project Co-ordinator in London for three years. She organises trips abroad for writers and has won two achievement awards for her work, *Cosmopolitan* magazine (1994) and *Candace* magazine (1996).

**john siddique...** 1964 – narrowmindedly optimistic obsessive big heart likes: avocados, olives, dub, samosas, ER loves and hates people allergic to cats eats too much bread writes books sometimes makes records sometimes http://users.netmatters.co.uk/jowonio_productions

Poet, songwriter, playwright, singer, musician, **Labi Siffre** is the writer and performer of the *Ivor Novello Award* winning song '(Something Inside) So Strong'. The writer of two volumes of poetry, *Nigger* and *Blood on the Page* (both published by Xavier Books) Labi Siffre has made a strong, and for many a disturbing, impact as a poet, "live" and on radio and TV.

**Lemn Sissay** has been published for approximately twelve years. His last book *Rebel Without Applause* came out six years ago. Between then and now he has been searching successfully for the closest members of his family. His next book *Morning Breaks in the Elevator* is due from Payback Press in February '99.

**Dorothea Smartt**, is of Barbajan heritage. Her poetryslide work *Medusa,* is a seminal Black performance work of the 1990's. A former Attached Live Artist at the Institute of Contemporary Arts, she's currently Brixton Market's Poet-in-Residence.

Previously published, London-based **Andria Smith** is one of the most exciting and respected female voices to emerge from the poetry scene in recent times.

**SuAndi** began writing sometimes, hopefully will not stop – stop – Tours nationally and internationally – stop – 4 solo publications, lots of anthologies and commissions – stop – Live artist – stop –Brosun inspired – stop

Bristol-born rapper and producer **Tricky** has released four solo albums and numerous collaborative projects. This collection includes lyrics from his albums *Maxinquaye, Pre-Millennium Tension* and *Angels with Dirty Faces.* He currently lives in New York.

London-based **Akure Wall** is currently working on her debut album, which is set for release shortly.

**Marie Guise Williams** writes poetry, short fiction, and has recently received a bursary from North West Arts towards the completion of her first novel. She describes her main objective as the dissection of sex, sexuality, race and gender, exploring the pains and pleasures which lie beneath the surface.